SECOND EDITION

Storybook 7

D0028260

The Sailboat Book

by Sue Dickson

Illustrations by Norma Portadino, Jean Hamilton, Chip Neville and Kerstin Upmeyer

Printed in the United States of America

Modern Curriculum Press, an imprint of Pearson Learning
299 Jefferson Road, P.O. Box 480, Parsippany, NJ 07054
1-800-321-3106 / www.pearsonlearning.com

ISBN: 1-56704-517-0 (Volume 7)

G H I J K L M N—CJK—05 04 03 02 01

Table of Contents

Raceway Step 19

most-frequently-used **sight words**	Page

Snacks for the Cubs **4**
by Vida Daly

Raceway Step 20

two-vowel words
ē¢/ ā/ĭ ē¢/ ō¢/

A Picnic on the Beach (Part 1) **19**
by Vida Daly

A Picnic on the Beach (Part 2) **30**
by Vida Daly

two-vowel words
+ silent
¢/

The Bike Hike and Dan's Cake **40**
by Vida Daly

The Bike Hike and Dan's Cake (Part 2) . . **47**
by Vida Daly

Fun on the Trail **54**
by Vida Daly

c = s

A Visit from Uncle Bruce **66**
by Hetty Hubbard

2

Snacks for the Cubs

Vocabulary

1. come
2. here
3. would
4. me
5. some
6. with
7. you
8. go
9. do
10. very
11. many
12. we

13. buy
14. when
15. for
16. any
17. love
18. all
19. see
20. may
21. one
22. three
23. seconds
24. new

25. what
26. look
27. from
28. two
29. our

Story Words

ba na nas
30. bananas

ap ple
31. apple

32. clock

33. o'clock

4

"Come here, Tom," said Mom. "Come here, Jim! Come here, Linda. Would you come to me?"

"We will go to the Snack
Hut," said Mom. "We will
buy some snacks. Come
with me."

"Here we come," said Jim
and Tom.

"Yes," said Linda. "We
like snacks. We will come
with you, Mom."

6

NUTS

"We do not have very many apples," said Jim. "We like apples. May we buy some?"

"Yes, I will buy some apples for you," said Mom.

"We do not have any nuts," said Jim. "We like nuts. May we buy some at the Snack Hut ?"

"Yes," said Mom. "We will buy some nuts."

"We do not have any pops," said Tom.

"We like pops," said Linda. "Will we buy some, Mom?"

"Yes, we will buy some pops," said Mom.

NUTS

"We do not have any bananas," said Linda.

"We like bananas," said Tom. "May we get some at the Snack Hut ?"

"Yes, we will buy some bananas," said Mom.

I just had the last one !

"May we get some hot dogs ?" said Linda. "We love hot dogs."

"Yes," said Mom. "We will get some."

"We will get to the Snack Hut in just three seconds," said Mom. "You will see some new snacks. You will get to pick some."

Snack Hut

OPEN

Lots of new snacks
YOU WILL LOVE!
COME AND PICK

Yum-yums   50¢

"What fun ! Look ! We can see the new snacks. What will we pick ?" said the cubs.

13

"I see nuts," said Tom.
"I am fond of nuts."

Mom said, "We can buy
two bags. Get two bags
from the box. Set two
bags in our basket."

14

Mom said to Jim, "See if you can get the pops. Look for a box with six pops in it."

"I can see one," said Jim, "but I have to dig for it."

POPS

"Do you see apples ?" said Mom.

"Yes, I do !" said Linda. "I see apples."

"May I get one apple for me, and one for Jim, and one for Tom ?" said Linda.

"No," said Mom. "One big bag will do."

Jim, Tom and Linda did help Mom. They did help Mom pick snacks. See the new snacks !

"It is three o'clock," said Mom. "We must go. We may have some of our snacks when we get back."

The Snack Hut was a lot of fun !

The End

Part 1
A Picnic on the Beach

Raceway Step 20A
two vowels
ēa̸ āi̸
ēe̸ ōa̸

Vocabulary

1. beach
2. heat
3. year
4. teach
5. deep
6. neat
7. sail
8. boat
9. sailboat
10. near
11. pail
12. eat
13. meal
14. lean
15. meat
16. green
17. beans
18. peach
19. peaches
20. cream
21. tea
22. pie
23. seat
24. clean
25. sea
26. weed
27. feet
28. wait
29. team
30. cheer
31. keep
32. feed
33. leap
34. three
35. float
36. ear
    ears

Story Words

can not
37. cannot
un til
38. until
39. would
40. could
41. said

19

"It is very hot," Mom said. "We will go to the beach. The heat will not be so bad at the beach."

"Yes, Mom," said Jack. "We love the beach."

"Yes, yes !" Sis said. "We do **love** the beach !"

20

"This year I will teach you to swim," said Mom, "but you must not go in very deep. Not yet. When you can swim, you may go in deep."

"But not yet," said Dad.

"I will set up the beach umbrella. It will help keep the sun from us," said Dad. "We cannot eat our meal in the hot sun. We will not eat yet."

22

"Come here, Sis," said Jack. "We can sail our sailboat. Come sail the boat with me. We will have fun."

"Look!" said Sis. "See the sailboat go from us. It will not go very deep. We will keep it near us. Look! See it sail!"

"One, two, three! **Go**, sailboat, **go**!" said Jack. "Our sailboat is a lot of fun."

"Come with me, Sis," said Mom. "See your new pail. You can get your new pail. You can fill it with sand. Your new pail will be fun."

25

"What will we do next?"
said Sis.

"We can eat our meal,"
said Mom. "We can have
a picnic. I have lean meat
and green beans for us."

26

"We have peaches and cream," Mom said. "We have tea and pie. Come sit on the mat. We will eat. This will be fun."

"We can have our
picnic on the beach," said
Jack. "Sis and I can sit
on the mat. Mom and
Dad can sit on a seat.
One, two beach seats,"
said Jack. "One seat for
Mom. "One seat for
Dad. Look! We can eat
our meal on the beach."

"That was fun," said
Dad. "Let us help Mom.
We can clean up the
mess. We must keep the
beach neat and clean.
Pack up the cups and tea
bags. Pack up the
napkins and the meat.
We will clean up from
the picnic."

The End

A Picnic on the Beach

"We can go up the beach," said Dad. "Let us see what we can do."

"We can feed the gulls on the beach," said Mom.

"We can see the swim team," said Jack.

"We can cheer for the team that wins," said Sis.

"See us do a leap frog," said Jack. "Sis and I can do a leap frog. Look, Mom ! Look, Dad ! We can do a leap frog in the sand. The beach is fun for us !"

31

"What do you see ?" said Mom.

"I see some seaweed," said Sis. "Look ! Lots of seaweed is on the beach."

"The sand is hot," said Jack. "The sand is very hot for my feet."

32

"You may get your feet wet," said Mom. "But do not go very deep."

"Will you teach us to swim?" said Sis.

"Not just yet," said Mom. "We must wait. We cannot swim until three o'clock. We just had our meal."

"We must wait," said Dad. "We can go back to sit on the beach mat to rest."

"OK," said Mom. "Get set ! It's three o'clock ! We can leap in ! One, two, three, leap in !

Leap in, Sis !

Leap in, Jack !

Leap in, Dad !"

Mom will teach Sis
to swim.

"Kick your feet," said
Mom. "Kick, and kick,
and kick !"

"See Dad float. Dad can float on his back! See Dad float!" said Mom.

"Teach **me** to float, Dad," said Jack.

"Keep your feet up," said Dad, "and let your ears get wet. Your feet must be up, and your ears must be in ! You can float, Jack !" See Jack float !

"We must go," said Mom. "Help me pack."

Dad will get the umbrella. Jack will get the beach seats. Sis will get the tea jug. Mom will get the beach mat.

"We had fun at the beach," said Sis.

"Yes, the beach is grand when the heat is bad," said Mom.

The End

The Bike Hike and Dan's Cake

Raceway Step 20B
two vowels
ēa̅ a̅i
ea̅ o̅a
and
silent e

Vocabulary

1. bike
2. like
3. take
4. hike
5. Jake
6. Mike
7. here
8. wave
9. cake
10. see
11. three
12. home
13. bake
14. rake
15. made
16. pile
17. pine
18. neat

19. came
20. fine
21. shade
22. feet
23. soak
24. cute
25. bee
26. peach
27. tree
28. keep
29. snail
30. creep
31. weed
32. goat
33. road
34. peep
35. five
36. seeds

37. green
38. need
39. spoke
40. wait
41. use
42. brain
43. chase
44. boat
45. time
46. rode
47. smile
48. face
49. leap

Story Words
lit tle
50. little
can dles
51. candles
52. pocket

40

"Would you like to take a bike hike ?" said Jake.

"Yes, I would," said Mike. "I will go ask my mom and dad if I may go."

"Yes, you may go on a bike hike," said Dad. "You may go with Jake, but you must be home at six o'clock. We will have a cake for Dan. It will have three candles. He will be three. Be home at six o'clock."

"OK, Dad. We will be home at six o'clock," said Mike. "We like cake. We like to see candles on a cake. We will get a gift for Dan."

"Here we go !" said Jake and Mike. "We will see you at six o'clock."

"Wave to Mike and Jake," said Dad. "They will come back to have cake with you, Dan. They will see your three candles, all lit up. It will be fun."

Mom went in to bake a cake for Dan. She will bake a big cake. Dan went with Mom. He will help Mom bake the cake.

Dad had to rake the grass. He made a big pile next to the pine tree.

"I hope I can get the pile of grass in this bag," said Dad. "I want it to look neat here. I want it neat by six o'clock."

The End (Part 1)

Part 2
The Bike Hike and Dan's Cake

Jake and Mike had a
fine bike hike. They had
a rest in the shade.
They sat by the pond to
rest. Mike stuck his feet
in the pond.

47

Jake said, "Look at that cute little duck."

"Yes, I see it," said Mike. "Do you see that bee by the peach tree?"

"Yes," said Jake. "Keep still ! See that snail creep up that weed ?"

Just as Jake spoke, Mike cried, "Look! A goat! I can hear a bell on his neck!"

"The goat with the bell did not scare that little robin," said Jake. "Just you !"

49

"I need a gift for Dan," said Mike.

All at once, a little frog went **leap** by the pond.

"I will creep up and get that frog," said Mike. "A little green frog will be a fine gift for Dan. He will like it."

"Wait," said Jake. "My brain tells me what we must do. We can get that frog if we chase him to that boat. One, two, three, **leap !** We got him ! Yippee !"

Mike kept the little green frog in his pocket. It was time to go home so Mike and Jake rode fast.

Dan did like his cake, and he did like his little green frog. "Thank you, Mike and Jake," said Dan. "Let's take 'Leap' to the pond. He will like it in the pond. Let's go !"

The End

Fun on the Trail

Vocabulary

two-vowel words

1. tail
2. trail
3. ear
4. east
5. road
6. cried
7. keep
8. clean
9. feel
10. Band-Aid
11. tree
12. trees
13. Dave
14. nose
15. hike
16. mile
17. take
18. drove
19. here
20. five
21. fine
22. time
23. pine
24. cone
25. cones

silent e̶

26. home
27. cure
28. nose
29. smile
30. vote
31. shade

Story Words

rab bit
32. rabbit
33. rabbits

be gin
34. begin
35. begins

let us
36. let's

54

Dave, Pat, and Meg
are rabbits.

Dave has a black spot
on his left ear. Pat has
a big pink nose. Meg
has a tail like a big puff
of fuzz.

Dave, Pat, and Meg
plan to go on a hike.
It will not be a little
hike. It will be a
big hike !

"We will go lots of miles. We must fill our back-packs. We must take the trail map," said Pat.

Dad and Mom drove Pat, Dave and Meg to the trail.

"The trail begins on East Hill Road," said Dad.

"Be back here by five
o'clock," said Mom.

"Fine. That will give us
lots of time," said Meg.

Up the trail they
went. It was very hot.
The shade of the trees
felt nice.

"See all the pine cones
on the trail," said Dave.
"Let's take some home
for Mom."

60

At the top of the hill
they sat to have a rest.

"Did Mom bake a cake
for us ?" said Pat.

"Yes," said Meg with a
smile. "It is in my
back-pack."

When the last bit of cake was gone, Pat cried, "Help! I have a bug bite on my nose!"

"I can cure it," said Dave. "Here is a Band-Aid from my kit. This will keep it clean. You will smile and feel fine in no time."

They had a big hike
and went lots of miles.

"Let's go back on the
same trail," said Pat.
"We will not get lost
on the same trail."

The rest of the hike
was just fine.

"The next time we go
on a hike, we will take
you, Dad," said Dave.

"Fine," said Dad.
"I vote for that!"

The End

65

Vocabulary

1. Grace	11. race
2. spice	12. once
3. nice	13. Alice
4. ice	14. trace
5. slice	15. place
6. Bruce	16. lace
7. face	17. price
8. twice	18. space
9. dice	Story Word
10. rice	po ta toes
	19. potatoes

"Mmmm," said Grace. "That spice cake smells nice, Mom. When will you ice it? I would like a slice."

"Not yet, Grace," said Mom. "Uncle Bruce will be here to have this meal with us. We will have to wait for him to come. We will cut the cake when he gets here."

"Let me help you get set for Uncle Bruce," said Grace.

Mom's face went into a big smile. "That will be nice, Grace. We can get set twice as fast if you help."

69

"Here, dice the potatoes, Grace. I will make the rice," said Mom.

Grace had a happy
face. She liked to clean
the rug. She got it nice
and clean.

"I will get Alice to help
us," said Grace. "We
can have a race."

Alice and Grace had a
race to dust and wax.
At last! Not a trace of
dust was in the place!

72

"Mom likes this lace one," said Alice. "Help me place it on the table, Grace."

Just then Joe came home. He held a nest in his hand.

"Mom, Mom, see what I have!" he said.

"That is nice, Joe," said Mom, "but you must place it back in the tree at once."

"Yes, Mom," said Joe.
"A nest is best in a tree.
The bird can come back
to the nest if it is in the
tree."

Joe was back fast. "Let me help you too, Mom," he said. "What can I do ?"

"You are nice, Joe," said Mom. "Yes, I can use your help."

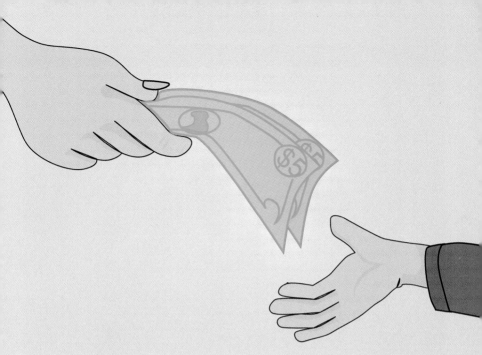

"You can buy the ice cream. Just tell me the price when you get back," said Mom.

"Mmm," said Joe. "Ice cream and spice cake!"

When Joe came back,
Mom said, "What a big
help you all are to me."

"Uncle Bruce will like
our place," said Alice.

"Yes," said Grace.

"He will love the ice cream and spice cake," said Joe, "and so will I. I have lots of space for it!"

"Yippee !" yelled Alice, Joe and Grace. "Uncle Bruce is here ! We can eat at last !"

The End